The Taming of the Shrew

A Shakespeare Story

RETOLD BY ANDREW MATTHEWS
ILLUSTRATED BY TONY ROSS

ORCHARD

For Jo, with love
A.M.

ORCHARD BOOKS
338 Euston Road, London NW1 3BH
Orchard Books Australia
Hachette Children's Books
Level 17/207 Kent St, Sydney, NSW 2000
First published in Great Britain in 2009
First paperback publication in 2010
This slipcase edition published in 2013
Not for individual resale
Text © Andrew Matthews 2009
Illustrations © Tony Ross 2009
ISBN 978 1 40780 975 5

A CIP catalogue record for this book is available from the British Library
Printed in China

Orchard Books is a division of Hachette Childrens Books,
an Hachette UK company.
www.hachette.co.uk

Contents

Cast List

Baptista
A rich gentleman
of Padua

Petruchio
A gentleman
from Verona

Lucentio
A young gentleman
from Pisa

Tranio
Lucentio's servant
and friend

Katherina
The shrew, Baptista's
daughter

Bianca
Katherina's young sister

Hortensio
A suitor to Bianca

Gremio
A suitor to Bianca

The Scene
Padua in the sixteenth century.

Her name is Katherina Minola
Renown'd in Padua for her scolding tongue.

Hortensio; I.ii.

The Taming of the Shrew

Baptista Minola was rich and respectable, but his two daughters were the talk of Padua. The younger, Bianca, was pretty, polite and modest. Her elder sister,

Katherina, was equally pretty, but her character was completely different. Gossips called her "the shrew", a nickname given to any woman with a quick temper and a sharp tongue. As a result, no suitor had asked Baptista's permission to marry Katherina. Bianca, on the other hand, had two suitors: the elderly but wealthy Gremio, and young Hortensio. Katherina was jealous of Bianca, and her jealousy made her more bad-tempered than ever.

One afternoon, two young men who were sightseeing in Padua happened to pass Baptista's house. One was dressed in colourful clothes. His name was Lucentio, the only son of the prosperous Pisan merchant Vincentio. Lucentio had arrived in Padua that morning, and planned to study at the university. The other young man was plainly dressed. He was Tranio, Lucentio's servant and close friend.

Both men were surprised when a door flew open, and Baptista burst into the street, followed by Gremio, Hortensio, Katherina and Bianca.

Baptista looked flustered. "You can't make me change my mind!" he said to Gremio and Hortensio. "Bianca won't

marry until Katherina has a husband.
I don't suppose either of you would
consider marrying her?"

"She's too fiery for me!" spluttered
Gremio. "Do you fancy taking her on,
Hortensio?"

"I would rather wrestle with a devil!"
Hortensio replied.

Katherina placed her hands on her hips, and glared at her father. "Are you going to let them insult me?" she shrieked.

"I hope you're satisfied, Katherina!" wailed Bianca. "Father is going to shut me away. I'll probably never marry, and it's all your fault!"

This outburst was too much for Baptista. "Enough!" he thundered. "Katherina, Bianca, go inside!"

Bianca burst into tears and fled indoors. Katherina sniffed defiantly, and followed her.

"You see the problem, gentlemen?" said Baptista. "If Bianca marries before her sister, Katherina will make my life a misery."

"Are you really going to shut Bianca away, Baptista?" enquired Hortensio.

"I am," said Baptista. "I must hire
a schoolmaster, and a music teacher
to educate her. If either of you hear of
someone suitable, please let me know."

Baptista returned to his house,
shaking his head and muttering to
himself.

Hortensio and Gremio exchanged cold glances. Then Hortensio sighed. "We have been rivals for Bianca's love," he said, "but perhaps we should join forces and find a husband for Katherina. Once she is married off, Bianca will be free to choose between us."

"That's a good idea!" agreed Gremio. "But what kind of fool would want to marry a shrew?"

The two suitors walked off together, deep in thought.

Tranio laughed aloud at the scene he had just witnessed. "I had no idea that Padua was so lively!" he giggled. "Did you notice the expression on the older sister's face?"

Lucentio appeared dazed. "I could only see Bianca!" he gushed. "Her sweet beauty! Her rosy lips! I must woo her!"

"How?" asked Tranio. "You heard her father. He won't let any suitors near Bianca until her sister is married."

"I've got it, Tranio!" cried Lucentio. "We're strangers here. Let's change clothes and places. You can pretend to be me, and ask permission to be Bianca's suitor.  Agree to anything, but make sure Baptista doesn't promise her to anyone else. I'll pretend to be a scholar, take the job as Bianca's teacher, and we'll get to know each other."

"And what then?" said Tranio.

Lucentio grinned. "And then love will find a way!" he said.

Hortensio returned home, and found an old friend waiting at his front door.

"Petruchio!" exclaimed Hortensio. "What brings you here from Verona?"

"I'm looking for a wealthy wife," Petruchio revealed. "I don't care what she is like, as long as she is rich."

Hortensio wasted no time. He told Petruchio about Katherina and Bianca.

"Hmm!" said Petruchio, with a gleam of interest in his eyes. "I know Baptista well – he is a friend of my father's – but I've never met his daughters. What is Katherina like?"

Hortensio pulled a face. "I won't lie to you. She is the worst shrew in Padua," he confessed.

"It will take more than harsh words to put me off!" Petruchio said. "I must see her at once!"

"Can I beg a favour of you?" pleaded Hortensio. "If I put on shabby clothes, will you recommend me as a music master to teach Baptista's daughters? Then I can woo Bianca in secret, while you woo Katherina."

Petruchio was about to agree when Gremio appeared with Lucentio, who was wearing Tranio's clothes and carrying a pile of books.

"I have found a scholar to tutor Bianca," announced Gremio.

"More importantly, my friend Petruchio here is willing to woo Katherina, and marry her, if her father gives her a large enough dowry," Hortensio said.

"Are you certain you want to woo
Katherina?" Gremio asked Petruchio.
"She's a wildcat!"

Petruchio thumped his chest. "I've faced
roaring lions, raging seas and booming
cannon!" he bragged. "I'm not afraid of
Katherina the shrew!"

"Excuse me?" said a voice. "Does anyone know where Bianca Minola lives?"

Everyone turned, and saw Tranio, dressed in Lucentio's finery. Lucentio winked slyly at his friend. "Who are you, and what is your business with Bianca?" demanded Hortensio.

"I am Lucentio, and I wish to woo her," Tranio lied smoothly.

Gremio turned red with rage. "Bianca is my chosen love!" he cried.

"Mine too!" added Hortensio.

"Gentlemen!" Petruchio said grandly. "You seem to forget that Bianca won't marry anyone, unless I marry Katherina. Your future happiness is in my hands!"

* * *

Not long afterwards, Baptista received
Gremio, Petruchio, Tranio – who was
passing himself off as Lucentio – and
the two so-called "scholars". After
introductions had been made, Baptista
sent the tutors away to begin teaching
his daughters.

Then Petruchio spoke boldly. "You know my father, Baptista, so you know the kind of  fellow I am. If I marry your daughter Katherina, what will her dowry be?"

"Twenty thousand crowns, and half my lands when I die," Baptista replied.

"Excellent!" said Petruchio. "The matter is settled."

Baptista smiled ruefully. "Getting Katherina to agree to the marriage might be more difficult than you think," he warned.

"I'll be more than a match for her!" Petruchio assured him. "I am the breeze that will cool her hot temper."

"Can I discuss Bianca's future with you now, Baptista?" ventured Gremio.

"And I!" broke in Tranio. "I am a newcomer to Padua, but I have already heard of Bianca's grace and beauty. I ask your permission to woo her, once Katherina is married." Before Baptista could answer, Hortensio staggered in, with his head sticking out from a broken lute.

"What happened to you?" gasped
Baptista.

"Katherina!" Hortensio groaned.
"When I told her she played badly, she
called me a twangling Jack, and smashed
this lute over my head." He wandered off
unsteadily.

"She's a lively one!" chuckled
Petruchio. "I'm longing to meet her!"

"I'll send her to you," said Baptista. "These two gentlemen and I have things to talk over." He led Gremio and Tranio into his study.

Once he was alone, Petruchio paced up and down. *I must confuse her with my wooing*, he told himself. *Whatever she says, I'll say the opposite, until she's so mixed up that she won't even notice I've married her!*

Katherina appeared, and for a moment Petruchio was struck dumb by her beauty, but he quickly recovered. "Good day, Kate," he said.

Katherina scowled. "No one calls me Kate!" she snapped.

"I'm going to," insisted Petruchio. "You are the prettiest Kate in the world. I shall marry you, and make you *my* Kate."

"Are you a madman who has wandered in off the street?" Katherina fumed.

"No, I'm a gentleman of Verona," declared Petruchio.

"We'll soon see if you're a gentleman!" snarled Katherina, and she slapped Petruchio's face.

Petruchio grabbed her by the wrists, and spoke softly to her while she struggled to escape. "I was told you had a bad temper, but you're as sweet as springtime flowers!" he cooed.

Katherina broke free. "You are mad!" she panted.

Baptista stepped out of his study. "How are you two lovebirds?" he asked.

"Do you really want me to marry this lunatic?" screeched Katherina. "What sort of father are you?"

"People are wrong to call your daughter a shrew, Baptista," Petruchio said. "They don't know the real Kate, the way I do. We've agreed to be married next Sunday."

"We haven't agreed anything!" yelped Katherina.

"I must go to Venice for my wedding outfit," Petruchio said. "Until Sunday, Kate." He blew her a kiss, and left; Katherina stormed off in the opposite direction.

Baptista returned to his study, where Gremio and Tranio were waiting.

"Bianca's happiness and comfort concern me most," he said to them. "For that reason, if you can prove your father is as wealthy as you claim, Lucentio, Bianca will be your wife."

Tranio bowed. "Thank you, sir," he said.

✳ ✳ ✳

On the following Sunday, Petruchio
continued with his scheme
to cure Katherina of
her shrewishness
by behaving
more
outrageously
than she
ever had.
He arrived late
at the church,
riding a scrawny
old horse, and
wearing a hat with
a ridiculously long
feather attached. His jerkin was patched,
his breeches were threadbare. One boot
was black, the other brown, and his
sword was bent and rusty.

During the ceremony, Petruchio bawled out his vows. The priest was so startled that he dropped his book, and when he stooped to pick it up, Petruchio boxed his ears, before insisting  on a goblet of wine, which he spilled over the priest's cassock. Finally, he kissed his new wife with a smacking sound that echoed through the church.

The moment the ceremony was over, Petruchio insisted that he and Katherina should journey to his house in Verona. By the time they got there, Katherina was tired and hungry, but when Petruchio's servants brought food, he said that she could not eat it because it was burnt.

When they went
to bed, he
rearranged
all the sheets
and pillows,
and was
continually
getting up to
open and
close the
windows,
first saying
that it was
too cold for
Katherina, and
then that it was
too stuffy. In the
end, Katherina was
too weary to complain.

* * *

The next morning, in the garden of
Baptista's house, Tranio and Hortensio hid
behind a shrub, and spied on Lucentio and
Bianca, who were seated side by side on a
bench.

"Look at how they're holding hands!"
whispered Hortensio. "See the way they're
gazing into each other's eyes? They're
madly in love. Fancy Bianca falling for a
penniless scholar!"

"She hasn't," Tranio confessed. "He is Lucentio. I'm his servant, Tranio. We swapped places so that he could woo Bianca."

"And he has won her!" sighed Hortensio. "Oh well! Actually, I've been pretending too. I'm not a music master, but Hortensio, a gentleman of Padua.

Since Bianca has given her heart to another, I'll be off. I know a pretty young widow who would marry me in the twinkle of an eye, if I asked her."

Hortensio was proved right, and within a few days, he married the widow, and Bianca married Lucentio – the real Lucentio.

* * *

A week later, Petruchio and Katherina
visited Padua to attend the party that
Baptista threw to celebrate his daughters'
marriages.

Though Katherina seemed less stubborn than she had been, Petruchio decided to annoy her, to test how well she could keep her temper. When they were almost at Baptista's house, he waved at the sky. "How brightly the moon shines!" he cried.

"The moon?" said Katherina, frowning. "That's the sun!"

"Well I say it's the moon!" Petruchio declared.

"And I know it's the sun!" retorted Katherina.

"So you still insist on contradicting me, eh?" Petruchio said. "Then let's go back to Verona. We can't stay at your father's house if we're going to bicker all the time."

Katherina hung her head. She was weary, hungry, thirsty, and had been looking forward to being reunited with her family. "All right, Petruchio!" she said meekly. "If you say it's the moon, then so it is."

"Ha, but I say it's the sun!" announced Petruchio.

"It can be a candle, if you like!" groaned Katherina. "I don't want to argue any more."

Petruchio beamed. "You have no idea how sweet those words sound!" he said.

As well as Bianca, Lucentio, Petruchio and Katherina, Hortensio and his bride were among the guests at the party. Towards the end of the evening, the three new husbands sat drinking together. Wine loosened their tongues and their wits, and they had a disagreement over whose wife was the most obedient.

"Let's settle the matter by each sending a servant to ask our wives to meet us here. The first wife to turn up will be the most obedient."

"Care to bet twenty crowns on the outcome?" asked Lucentio.

"My Katherina is worth more than a bet of twenty crowns!" Petruchio protested.

"A hundred, then?" suggested Lucentio.

"Done!" agreed Petruchio. "You go first."

Lucentio beckoned to a servant. "Tell your mistress I want to see her right away," he said.

The servant promptly left the room, and soon returned. "My mistress says she is too busy to come to you now, sir," he told Lucentio.

Petruchio and Hortensio sniggered at Lucentio's blush.

"Go and ask my wife to come to me!" Hortensio instructed the servant. Once again the servant left, and once again he returned alone.

"Your wife says she is in no mood for jokes, sir," he informed Hortensio. "If you wish to see her, you must go to her."

It was Hortensio's turn to blush.

"Tell Mistress Katherina I wish to see her," Petruchio said to the servant.

For the third time, the servant left, and before long Katherina appeared. "You sent for me, husband?" she said.

"Yes," replied Petruchio. "Find Bianca and Hortensio's wife, and fetch them here."

Katherina did as she was told, and within a minute, all three wives stood before their husbands.

"Now, Kate," Petruchio said. "Tell these two headstrong women what you have learned about husbands and wives."

"Our husbands keep us warm and safe, and work hard to feed and clothe us," began Katherina, "so we should love, honour and obey them – not scold them.

We are softer and weaker than men, and it's foolish to squabble with them. Husbands and wives should take delight in one another."

Petruchio laughed, and held out his hand to Katherina. "No one will ever call you a shrew again!" he promised. "Come here and kiss me, Kate!"

Why, there's a wench! Come on and kiss me, Kate.

Petruchio; V.ii.

Love and Marriage in The Taming of the Shrew

Though no one is entirely certain, most scholars agree that Shakespeare probably wrote *The Taming of the Shrew* some time between 1593 and 1596. He seems to have taken some of the plot from *Supposes* by George Gascoigne (1566), and may also have been inspired by the ballad *A Shrewd and Cursed Wife* (1550).

Views on marriage have obviously changed a great deal from Shakespeare's time, when a good wife was expected to be meek and obedient, and the husband was very much the head of the household. Today, many would be sympathetic towards the feisty Katherina, and would feel uncomfortable about the way Petruchio subdues her.

However, the play is a comedy, and it is difficult to take it seriously, because Shakespeare exaggerates things until they become ridiculous. Katherina is a fire-breathing dragon of a shrew – sharp-tongued, vicious and violent. Petruchio is a posturing macho-man with preposterous self-confidence, and some of the methods he uses to tame Katherina are downright silly. Lucentio glimpses Bianca in the street, and instantly falls madly in love.

Shakespeare blends their stories into a frothy mixture of disguises, misunderstandings and romance. As in a pantomime, the audience is never in any doubt that the drama will end happily.

Shakespeare and the Globe Theatre

Some of Shakespeare's most famous plays were first performed at the Globe Theatre, which was built on the South Bank of the River Thames in 1599.

Going to the Globe was a different experience from going to the theatre today. The building was roughly circular in shape, but with flat sides: a little like a doughnut crossed with a fifty-pence piece. Because the Globe was an open-air theatre, plays were only put on during daylight hours in spring and summer. People paid a penny to stand in the central space and watch a play, and this part of the audience became known as 'the groundlings' because they stood on the ground. A place in the tiers of seating beneath the thatched roof, where there was a slightly better view and less chance of being rained on, cost extra.

The Elizabethans did not bath very often and the audiences at the Globe were smelly. Fine ladies and gentlemen in the more expensive seats sniffed perfume and bags of sweetly scented herbs to cover the stink rising from the groundlings.

There were no actresses on the stage; all the female characters in Shakespeare's plays would have been acted by boys, wearing wigs and make-up. Audiences were not well behaved. People clapped and cheered when their favourite actors came on stage; bad actors were jeered at and sometimes pelted with whatever came to hand.

Most Londoners worked hard to make a living and in their precious free time they liked to be entertained. Shakespeare understood the magic of the theatre so well that today, almost four hundred years after his death, his plays still cast a spell over the thousands of people that go to see them.

Orchard Classics

Shakespeare Stories

RETOLD BY ANDREW MATTHEWS
ILLUSTRATED BY TONY ROSS

Orchard Books are available from all good bookshops.